LORD CHANGE MY VIEW

SEEING LIFE FROM GOD'S PERSPECTIVE

II

LORD CHANGE MY VIEW

SEEING LIFE FROM GOD'S PERSPECTIVE

JEAKETA MANGA

Destiny Group Publishing
Chesterfield, Virginia

IV

LORD CHANGE MY VIEW

ISBN **978-0-9845732-0-2**

Lord Change My View

Published by Destiny Group Publishing

Chesterfield, VA 23832

Cover Design: Lamont Caleb Coward

VI

ACKNOWLEDGEMENTS

First, I would like to give honor and glory to **God**. I would have never been able to imagine the creativity you placed inside of me. Thank you for loving me and saving me from myself.

I would like to say a special thank you to my husband, Kennedy. I know that there are so many great things in you that are coming forth in due season. Thank you for pushing me. I love you and I am truly blessed to be your wife. Thank you Kaitlyn, for taking naps to allow mommy time to finish this project, I love you baby girl.

I would like to say thank you to my parents, Harold James Jr and Jean Dixon. God has used you in a special way; no one else can be my Mom and Dad. Thank you for everything.

I thank God for my pastors, Bishop Daniel and Co-Pastor Elena Robertson. They have shown me that age does not predict what we can accomplish when we put our trust in God. Bishop thank you for your no nonsense approach to bringing the word. Thank you Co-Pastor for always showing me how to be a woman of excellence, I pray that God will continue to bless your lives for everything you give.

A special thank you to my father-in-law, Papa, you possess so much wisdom Man of God, I thank God that He allowed you to come into my life. Thank you for taking the time to help me with this book.

VIII

FOREWARD

We are all products of our environments. The people, places, and things that surrounded us as we were growing up influenced our course of development in becoming who we are today. Some have experienced constructive reinforcements to become the very best that they could be. On the other hand, others' have suffered through negative and discouraging environments. Whether, negative or positive, our environments have affected how we see ourselves and others around us.

How do you see yourself? How do you see others? Can you clearly see what lies ahead of you? It's all in your perception. Jeaketa Manga, in her book, "Lord Change My View" has cleverly captured the essence of what perception is all about. As a skilled optometrist, Jeaketa explains what perception is, how it affects you, and how to adjust your perception in order to travel the road of success.

I am one of the millions of people across the world that has to use prescription glasses or contact lenses to help correct my vision. I have alternated between wearing glasses and contacts for years. These prescriptions have only served as a temporary solution. I finally decided after much research to go through laser eye surgery to help to correct my vision on a more permanent basis. It significantly changed my life. This procedure enabled me to see with 20/20 vision. As you read, allow Jeaketa to serve as your spiritual optometrist, to check your vision and diagnose what corrective treatment you need in order to see with 20/20 vision.

Co-Pastor Elena Robertson

Mt. Gilead Full Gospel Int'l Ministries

Table of Contents

WHAT DO YOU SEE?

In my first year in college, during my basic drawing class, we were given an assignment where we were required to sit outside of the classroom and draw everything we could see from that spot. This included the wall, the ceiling, the inside of the classroom and even the people that sat in front of you. What I found interesting about this assignment was the fact that when you looked at your drawing alone, you could only see things from your own point of view. However, when you looked at another person's drawing, each person portrayed something different. I found it amusing how a group of people sitting outside of the same classroom saw things in different ways. The outcomes of most of our assignments were the same in this drawing class.   People had their own ways of interpreting what the teacher asked for.   I have learned since then, that this is how people view life. They have different perspectives which shape their perceptions.   And that can be a result of their environment, attitudes, and upbringing. So in essence, if we are not open to other perspectives, then we are unable to think beyond our own perceptions.

So that you will understand what I am talking about let's look at the words closely. The definition of the word *perspective* is to look through or see clearly. *Perception* means to achieve the understanding of something. The way you see things, your perspective, directly affects your understanding of those things which in turn is your perception. The two words sound the same and it is because they are related and both affect your walk with God. Matthew 6:22-23 says that, *"The light of the body is the eye: if therefore thine eye be single, thy whole body shall be full of light. However, if thine eye be evil, thy whole body shall be full of darkness. If therefore the light that is in thee be darkness, how great is that darkness?"* This scripture is explaining that your eyes are the windows to your soul. If you are seeing things the right way, then you will perceive or do the right things. On the other hand, if your perspective is not right, then you perceive things the wrong way.

So with that being said, what are you seeing from your view? Are you willing to look at things another way? Do you take chances and go beyond your scope of understanding? Try it sometimes to see what happens. What would happen if we open ourselves up to God and allow Him to show us things from His perspective? He can definitely help us to see things clearly.

There was a blind man who walked with Jesus out of town. This man had been this way all of his life. Jesus spat on the ground, mixed it with dirt, and then put the mud on the man's eyes. His sight was restored immediately. Once the man's eyes were opened, he told Jesus he saw men walking as trees. He could see, but not clearly. However once Jesus laid his hands on the man he was able to see everything (Mark 8:23-25). This man was never able to see and then all of a sudden Jesus uses an unorthodox way of restoring his sight. If He can do that, imagine what He has in store for us. If we allow God to change our outlook we will be able to see things the way He does.

Let me help you understand what I mean. Have you ever taken the time to sit down and think about some of the things from which God has delivered you? When you are going through something, it can feel like the worst thing in the world at the time, but when you come out of it you notice that it was not as bad as it seemed. You may even find yourself laughing at the way you reacted. I remember a time where I had to trust God, and allow Him to change my perspective and perception of the direction of my life. I was dating a young man who was nice and well respected by his peers, the members of his church and even my family. We dated for two and a half years. Anyone would think that we were definitely a match made in heaven. And he was a great person, however, our conversations most of the time would end in arguments, because we could not agree on key issues. We both had different ideas of how we were to receive the word and how to walk it out daily. We were not even able to agree on the church we would attend. It was pretty bad. We continued the relationship and in spite of the telltale signs, we headed in the direction of marriage. God was trying to show me all the signs that this man was not the husband He chose for me, but I could not see beyond my current perspective. He was a nice person, the family loved him, and we looked great together. I made no reference to his relationship with God, because it looked good. In essence, I was looking at our relationship from the wrong perspective and relying on other people's perceptions. My whole family loved him and my uncle told me on several occasions he was proud of my choice in a mate. Every time, I tried to make a conscious decision to leave the relationship, I would worry about what people would think and how much it would hurt him. I did not understand at that time how important it was for God to be who I thought of first. I was miserable. It was not until I was completely weary of the arguments, that I sought God's perfect will for my life. I finally ended the relationship with a lot of prompting from God. At the time, walking away from him was the most painful thing I ever had to do. But once it was over, I was able to look in from the outside. I was able to see that this man's assignment clearly could have never matched the one God gave me. We were very good friends from the beginning, but that was all we were supposed to be.

I found that, if I kept viewing that relationship from my own from my own perspective, I would have missed the real assignment God had for me. Now do you see how important it is to look at things from God's point of view? If I were not obedient to His voice, I would have married this man only to find out that he was the wrong one. That would have been a disaster. So think about it again. Where in your life have you not submitted to God's view of your life? It is critical for us to do that. Sometimes our perspective can leave us blind to what God's will. We focus on what we want at that particular time and forget to ask God what he truly wants for us. We then expect God to fix things that would have never happened.

This book will help us to understand how to look at our life from God's perspective and allow His perception to rule in us. It is essentially vital in our walk with Christ, that we see things His way. We are going to look at how you view yourself, situations, others, and ultimately how you see God. So sit back, relax, and enjoy the pages of this book. Let it change your life the way it has changed mine. Allow God to open your eyes to what He wants you to see. God bless you.

I.

How do you view

yourself?

Chapter One

"Before I formed you in the womb I knew and approved of you as My chosen instrument, and before you were born I separated and set you apart, consecrating you; and I appointed you as a prophet to the nations".(Jeremiah 1:5)

God created us before we were ever thoughts in our mothers' minds. He knew exactly what He wanted from us. He knew the color of our skin, eyes, and hair. He even knew what imperfections we would have before we did. He loved us in spite of ourselves. So the question becomes, what do you feel about you? It is very important to be able to answer this question. The way you see yourself determines how you perceive yourself. The word of God states that, "As a man thinks in his heart so is he" (Proverbs 23:7). Therefore, whatever you think about yourself that is how you feel about you. It is the way you think you are. If your thinking is skewed for any reason, it will give you the wrong view of yourself. God created us the way He wanted us to be, however, we spend a lot of time trying to change what He has done. We forget to be happy with ourselves the way that we are. When you have a healthy relationship with yourself, you are able to enjoy and appreciate life. You take the time to smell the flowers and just enjoy being you. You find yourself thanking God for who He is and who He created you to be and not for what He does for you. So, how do you see yourself? What feelings do you have about how God has created you? What feelings do you have about why He created you? Most of the time those answers come from the way you were taught to think about yourself, whether it was good or bad. Our perspective of ourselves can come from the way we were raised and how we perceived our childhood. Laurie Ashner and Mitch Meyerson said it best, "the way you viewed things in your early years, really shapes your thoughts and feelings about who you are ". For example, if you grew up in a neighborhood in a two-story house with blue shutters and a white picket fence with both parents, you may see things a lot differently than another person, who only saw a wire fence

from a two-story apartment building living with grandparents.

Maybe your parents, or guardians, told you everyday how

much they loved you and how wonderful you were. On the

other hand, maybe they criticized you and told you there was

nothing good about you. No matter what happened, it affected

you, positively or negatively. And what you took away from

that experience determines how you feel. In my own life, I

faced feelings of insecurity, rejection, and unworthiness. These

feelings occurred during my teenage years and continued into

adulthood. I felt like I was unimportant and burdensome to

others. It consumed me. Every time I would think of things I

wanted to do, I would be too afraid to move forward thinking

that I did not have what it took. However, as a young child, I

felt like I could do anything. I had so much confidence. I

wanted to be a dancer, singer, songwriter, artist, novelist,

gymnast, and fashion designer. I wanted it all and you could

not tell me I was going to fail. I was unstoppable. God wants

us to be like that. He wants us to look at things, as if we are children (see Mark 10:15, Luke 18:17). He wants us to feel like we can do anything through Him. That is where we receive our dreams. He gives them to us. That is why children can easily tell you what they want to do when they get older. It is only when we do not allow those dreams God gave us to materialize for whatever reason, do we lose confidence in our abilities and ourselves. After awhile, I did lose that confidence. I started to allow the enemy to steal the zeal I once had for everything. I did not feel that I could be what God had called me to, based on the success of my family. None of them ever fulfilled their dreams. Whenever I expressed my dream to any of them, they would make me feel like it was not possible. I did not fault them for feeling that way because they had never seen real success. They only taught me what they learned. It was not until I came into the household of faith that I realized I could do everything God created me to do. I learned that faith is not only believing the impossible, but seeing the impossible through God's perspective. I was allowing fear to stop me and perceiving things with my limited understanding. I had to choose which way I was going to go. It was up to me to realize that God is a big God and with Him anything is possible (see Matthew 19:26). I began to regain that confidence I once had.

Confidence is the key to your success in who God has called you to be. Hebrews 10:35 states, *"Cast not away therefore your confidence, which hath great recompense of reward."* God gives you confidence and your reward is fulfilling your true call and destiny. Have you noticed if you are not fulfilling that call, there is an unrest that follows you? But do you feel that you are unable to fill the shoes that God wants you to fill? This is totally normal. It is only when you refuse to move that you continue to lack that confidence. Now please understand that I am talking about assurance that comes from God, not you. If you look throughout the Bible, God did not choose those who were so confident in themselves. If that were true then God could not have used those men. He is not able to gain glory through someone who is overly self-confident. If that was the case, men would always take the credit. God used men who relied heavily upon Him, and would bring Him the glory. Let us look at the story of Moses, and other influential men in the Bible. They can help add some insight to how we perceive ourselves.

Chapter Two

"Come now therefore, and I will send thee unto Pharaoh, that thou mayest bring forth my people the children of Israel out of Egypt (Exodus 3:10).

Moses was born during the time when the Egyptians were oppressing the children of Israel. Pharaoh ordered all Hebrew male babies put to death, so that they would not grow up and try to take over Egypt. He wanted to make sure that the Israelites remained slaves (See Exodus 1:8-22). Moses was born to a Hebrew woman who went to great lengths to protect him. She sent him away so that he would live. Although he was born a slave, Moses was found by Pharaoh's daughter and she took him in as her son (Exodus 2:10). When the time came for Moses to fulfill his call, God spoke to him. Now this came after an incident that made him feel unworthy of what God required. Moses tried to reason with God and came up with excuses as to why he could not do this great thing. One of the main things he argued was that he was not an eloquent speaker, but God had already planned for that. God already had the answer before He told Moses the plan. Aaron was in position to assist him with the people.

God knew what He put in Moses and everything he needed to complete his assignment was there. Even when Moses wanted to know how this thing could be done, God had the answer. He let Moses know that he would not be going in his own name, but in God's name (Exodus 3:14-15). That gave Moses the confidence to step outside of himself and let God have His way. Even though God told Moses to go to Pharaoh and tell him to free the Israelites, he hardened Pharaoh's heart each time. God used this situation to build Moses' confidence. If Moses had not seen the works of God before leading the people out of Egypt, he would never have believed that God could use him. His confidence in God kept him while he fulfilled the call. Each time God sent Moses to Pharaoh, He helped Moses to see what He promised.

That is how we feel about ourselves. We allow the way we feel about our weaknesses, predict how we carry out our lives. I am able to identify with Moses in the fact that I let my weaknesses cloud my vision. I would focus on my mistakes and allow them to hold me back from being confident in God. I realized that others could see the potential in me, but when I looked, I saw failure. I, just like Moses, was afraid to claim what was rightfully mine. Instead of looking at all the great qualities God has given me, I focused on everything that was wrong with me. My skin was too dark, my hair was not pretty and long, my legs were too skinny, and the list continued. I even felt sorry for myself about the way that I had to grow up dealing with issues on my own because my mom was not in a position to teach me how to be a young lady. I would always look at others and feel like they were better than I was. Not that this was the case, but that was the way I felt. I didn't focus on the beautiful singing voice, warm smile, or creative mind he had given me. It took years before I was able to really let God use those attributes.

Take for instance the gift of ministering in song. Before I was able to step out to allow God to use my voice, I would cower and cringe anytime I stood before people to sing. I would cry from nervousness. I almost dropped the microphone a few times, because I was shaking so hard. I began to notice that no matter how fearful I was God always gave me more opportunities to sing in front of others. It was not until I realized that it was not about me, that I began to step out confidently. He still surprises me every time I get up to minister, if I let Him take control.

David said it best in Psalms 139, when he said that God even knows the thoughts that we are thinking before we think them. Why would you rely on your own understanding of who you are, without looking to God to gain insight as to how He created you? He made you fearfully and wonderfully (see Psalms 139:14). He put His words in your mouth (see Jeremiah 1:9) He wrote your book! I always tell my husband that whenever there is a defect with the product, you must go back to the manufacturer. If you want to get past the negative feelings you have about your life, mistakes, and actions, go back to God. God does not look at all of that, but He pays close attention to your heart. He is a merciful God, who would not count all those things against you. David was another one of the great men of God in the Bible, but he had so many issues you would not even believe it until you read it in the Bible. The thing that I admire so much about David was that he was a man after God's own heart and anytime he was wrong, he went back to God and repented. He was able to win battles because he moved when God told him to move, and when he fell short, he still went back to God to wait for further instructions. He always went back to God to gain the right perspective.

Therefore, you see not even the great men of the Bible were perfect. Again, God does not call you because you do not have any issues. He does not call you because you are perfect. Moses killed a man before he was set to fulfill his destiny. He ran away because he did not see any worth in himself. God did not care about that. He sent Jesus come to wash us clean of all of our shortcomings. He wants you and your issues so that He can use your testimony to set someone else free. The word says "And they overcame him by the blood of the Lamb and by the word of their testimony..." (Revelation 12:11). Your life, mistakes included, is all a part of God's great testimony. Yes, I said God's testimony. He gets all the glory for everything that we are. So start looking at yourself the way God sees you. If you make a mistake, do not worry about it, He knew you would. If we get to the point where we know that this is all God and none of us, we will look at things His way. If we put our focus on Him, we would not have a problem doing anything He asks us to do. David longed for God, because God was all that he had. Psalm 42:1 states, *"As the hart panteth after the water brooks, so panteth my soul after thee, O God."* Do you know how thirsty deer are when they are panting? Think about how you feel when you are extremely thirsty or dehydrated. That is serious. If we long for God that way, we would not allow anything we feel keep us from pleasing him. God knows what we are capable of doing and what we are not. He knows everything about us and the call placed on us. He even knows that we will hesitate when He tells us it is time to do what He tells us. We just have to change the way we perceive things. Let God show you what He already planned for you to do. Just allow Him the freedom to control the way you feel about yourself. It will even change the way you look at the circumstances in your life.

Part One Discussion Questions

(Chapters 1 & 2)

Please answer all questions completely. They are designed to help you and will only be beneficial if you answer truthfully.

1) How do you see yourself? Is it positive or negative? How do you plan to change your outlook? (Choose scriptures and explain how you will apply them).

2) If you could change one thing about yourself, what would it be? Why would you like to change it? Do you feel like it would change the way you see yourself?

3) Where do you feel that the opinions you have about yourself come from? Is it based on what you have or have not accomplished?

4) What has God called you to do? Are you fulfilling that call or in the process of doing so? Do you believe what the word says about what He's called you to do?

5) Do you feel like you can identify with the struggles that Moses endured while stepping out to do what God told him to do? (Yes or no and why)

II.

How do you view

your circumstances?

Chapter Three

"Not that I speak in respect of want: for I have learned, in whatsoever state I am, therewith to be content." (Philippians 4:11)

How do you view a glass of water filled half way? Do you see it as being half-empty or half full? Your answer to this question determines the perspective in which you perceive your circumstances. We are all human and our feelings determine our reaction to situations. Proverbs 3:5-6 lets us know that if we trust in God with everything that we are, then He will show us the way. He will help us when we do not understand. That is why the word states "not to lean to your own understanding". It will not lead you where God wants you to go. And, if you read further down to Proverbs 3:8, it says that if you trust God it is healthy for you. In the previous chapter, we talked about how it is good to have healthy thoughts about yourself; the same is true for your circumstances. God wants us to look at our situations the right way as well.

Have you ever thought that you could have had a better car, lived in a better home, or obtained a better job? How do you feel about your life? Do you think that if you could reverse some of the things that happened, you would have lived better? If your answer was yes to most of those questions, do not feel bad, mine too. I thought that if both my parents had been around when I was growing up, I would not have felt rejection or pain. I thought things would have been perfect if my family had been more positive, and not so discouraging. The truth of the matter is, I do not know how things would have been if the tables were turned. I was too busy looking at where I could have been or what I could have had, instead of why I should be thankful. Although, I may not have had everything I needed all the time, I still had a lot to be grateful for even back then. In Philippians 4:6 Paul says, *"Be careful for*

nothing; but in everything by prayer and supplication with
thanksgiving let your requests be known unto God."

He also said that no matter what state he was in, he learned to be content. That is a lot considering he was in jail, he was persecuted, and continuously being chased by the religious rulers. He was an ex-Pharisee, who let the power of God change his entire being. If you know anything about the Pharisees and Sadducees in the Bible, they were the religious men who served in the temples. They were well acquainted with the laws of following God, but had no clue about the Spirit of God. They were known for persecuting the followers of Christ. Paul oversaw the stoning of Stephen, one of the Apostles who preached about the goodness of the Lord, and sought to kill others (see Acts 7-8). He was on his way to Damascus to search for more Apostles, when Jesus met him on the road. The light of Jesus blinded his eyes and asked him why he was persecuting these people (see Acts 9). Once he experienced that personal encounter with Jesus, his life was changed forever. He wrote most of the New Testament. An ex-Pharisee credited with most of the New Testament of the Bible. Wow! He followed Jesus and was more on fire for that cause than he was for the title he previously carried.

What would happen if we could be that way? Do you think Paul had time to sit and think about the sins of his past? Or what things he could have done differently? That would have taken the rest of his life. The word states that "God blots out all of our sins and remembers them no more" (see Isaiah 43:25). So why do we sit and think on those things? If God forgets them why should we remember? I used to think that I could not be successful because of the way I grew up. It took me so many years to stop blaming my family for my life. I lost so much time I could have been working on other things. What I did find is that even if you have both parents and a good upbringing, it does not mean that things will always turn out great. Even if you live in a nice house and the best neighborhood, you have to make the right choices in order to succeed. The way you perceive your situation, determines the decisions you make for you own life, not the situation itself. One of my friends had the life I thought I needed to succeed. His parents were teachers, had a great marriage, and both on fire for God. It was the perfect setup, or so I thought. I saw parents who just wanted their son to go in the right direction and gave him the space to choose his way. He did not see things that way. He saw parents that tried to push him into church and always tell him what to do. He did not want his friends to think that he was not cool, so he did illegal things to prove to them that he was. He saw his circumstance as a hindrance to the life he thought he wanted. He wanted to appear tough and fit in with the crowd, not to be seen as a goody two shoes. I saw the same situation as the family I always wanted. I grew up in a household with extended family because my father was in the military, so I rarely saw him, and my mother was dealing with her own issues. After I turned ten, my mother found herself in a rough situation. She turned to substances to soak away the pain of her choices. As a result, I stayed with my relatives. I did not hear a lot of the positive things a child needed to hear or experience a healthy environment. Don't get me wrong, the house was clean and well kept, but the encouragement was lacking. After we graduated, I went on to college to further my education, but my friend ended up spending the rest of his life in prison. Now I know that this was a drastic example, and not everyone who rebels against their parents will deal with this. However, that whole situation really opened my eyes. I understood that no matter what your circumstances are, you determine your outcome. You have to choose whether to follow God's direction or your own, not your circumstances. In Proverbs 19:21 Solomon states that, *"Many plans are in a man's mind, but it is the Lord's purpose for him that will stand."* Therefore, no matter what your circumstance, God is greater than anything you have ever gone through. Your history, whether good or bad, does not hinder the plan of God. He gives you the free will to choose the way.

As Paul stated, in whatever state you are in, you can be content. It does not matter what happened to you in the past. It does not predict your future. You have to take a stand and start looking at your circumstances from God's view. 2 Kings 6:16-17 states, "*Elisha answered, 'Fear not; for those with us are more than those with them'. Then Elisha prayed, 'Lord, I pray you, open his eyes that he may see'. And the Lord opened the young man's eyes...*" The young man was seeing their circumstances the wrong way. He was seeing all that was against them. Elisha wanted to get God's perspective so he asked the Lord to show the young man what He saw. He knew that in order for God to deliver them from that mountain, they had to be in agreement with God's perception of the situation. God sees the big picture. He sees your end from the beginning. That is why He asks us to trust him with our whole heart. He knew that you would go through everything you have experienced in your life. He promised that He would always be there (Hebrews 13:5). However, if we continue to look at things as if there is no hope, things will not be good. He let us know in

Jeremiah 29:11 that he knows the thoughts and plans he thinks toward us and He already has our expected end in mind. God knows how to turn any situation around, especially if it is meant to cause you harm. Remember, He wrote your entire life story. He chose your family and then chose how you would live.

Chapter Four

"...You intended to harm me , but God intended it for good to accomplish what is now being done, the saving of lives" *(Genesis 50:20).*

Let us look at the story of Joseph, another of God's favored men in the Bible. He was born into a family of twelve brothers. He was the eleventh son of Israel. Israel was the son of Isaac, and the grandson of Abraham. Joseph was so different from the rest of his brothers. He was an ambitious young man, who God entrusted with prophetic dreams, the ability to interpret those dreams, and the gift of leadership and administration. He was Israel's favorite; because out of all the wives he had, Joseph was the firstborn to Rachel, the wife he truly loved (see Genesis 37:3). His brothers knew that their father preferred him over the rest of them and hated him for that reason (see Genesis 37:19-20). Joseph made the mistake of sharing his dreams with his brothers. God showed Joseph in his dreams that he was to rule over his entire family. After hearing those dreams, his brothers plotted to kill him. However, instead of taking his life, however, they decided to sell him to the Egyptians as a slave. They lied to their father, making him believe that an evil beast killed Joseph (Genesis 37:32-33). This separated Joseph from his family for 13 years and changed his life forever. He went from being favored in his father's sight to a slave in Egypt. Although to some it may have seemed tragic, it propelled him straight into his destiny. He may have looked at his circumstance as an end to his life at the time, but God never left him. Reading further about Joseph, you will see that the same favor his father showed him (God's favor), he received until he died. Therefore, you see, although Joseph's brothers sold him into slavery, God still saw him as a king. He was an overseer in Potiphar's home, jail, and then eventually over the entire well-being of Egypt (see Genesis 39-41). If Joseph spent too much time looking at his circumstances, he would have missed his appointment with destiny. I truly believe that Joseph may have cried for a moment, and then stopped focusing on what his brothers did to him. When given the opportunity to confront his brothers again, he did not remind them of what they did to him. It hurt him that his brothers' plot changed his entire life, but he forgave them (see Gen 42-44). They worried that he would avenge himself but Joseph said to them, *"'Fear not: for am I in the place of God? As for you, you thought evil for me, but God meant it for good, to bring about that many people should be kept alive, as they are this day. Now therefore, do not be afraid. I will provide for and support you and your little ones'. And he comforted them and spoke kindly to them."* (Genesis 50:21)

If we can look at our circumstances from the perspective that Joseph chose to view his, we can overcome anything that the enemy uses to distract us. He let them know that what you meant for bad, God turned it around for His glory. Tell those circumstances, that God has a plan for you, and they will not hold you captive. I learned that I did not have to feel bad about my circumstances and that I could experience true joy. My bishop stated in a sermon, "Who told you that you had to fix everything? Give it to God!" I know that those things may have hurt you deeply, but we have to let them go. Let the Lord reveal the joy you already possess and stop letting circumstances re-kindle the pain. The word of God in Nehemiah 8:10 states, that the joy of the Lord is your strength. How can we experience true joy from the inside if our circumstances are still in our view? How can God show us what He has for us, if we are still looking at what we could have had? Ask yourself these questions and be real with yourself about the answers. If you choose your circumstances over God, you are fighting a losing battle. Looking at things from God's view is like driving in total darkness with your high beams on. You can see everything in front of you, but there is nothing but darkness behind you. If you are looking back at your circumstances, you cannot see what is ahead. You lose focus when you look from the perspective of your circumstances, and you always perceive yourself as you did before. For a moment, you see yourself in God's eyes, but if the enemy brings any circumstance to your remembrance, you forget who you are. Like the word states in James 1:23-24; "*For if any be a hearer of the word, and not a doer, he is like unto a man beholding his natural face in a glass: For he beholds himself, and goes his way, and straightway forgets what manner of man he was.*"

You do not have to be that way. I began to thank God for everything that happened to me. I stopped regretting and started truly enjoying my life. I also learned not to blame the people involved in the circumstances. If you keep doing that you never assume responsibility for your own life. You constantly make excuses as to why things did not happen the way you wanted them to. Remember, you are responsible for fulfilling your own destiny. God will show you the way if you allow Him to, but you have to take the first step. If you let him help you, He will show you that you are in control of the way you view yourself, circumstances, and ultimately others.

Part Two Discussion Questions

(Chapters 3 & 4)

Please answer all questions completely. They are designed to help you and will only be beneficial if you answer truthfully.

1) How do you view a half-filled glass of water? Do you see it as half full or half empty?

2) How can you apply Philippians 4:11 to your everyday life and circumstances?

3) How do you handle your past issues? Do you deal with them or do you let them go and hope they will go away?

4) Do you compare yourself with others? If so, why?

5) How has God used your past or present circumstances to mature you? How has He used them to help others?

III.

How do you view

others?

Chapter Five

"Thus says the Lord; cursed is the man that trusts in man, and makes flesh his arm and whose heart departs from the Lord."

(Jeremiah 17:5)

Have you found yourself thinking more about how people see you than you are about God's opinion of you? Do you find yourself leaning heavily on man's perspective and perception? Do you find yourself changing your opinion or perception of things based on the opinions and views of others? If the answer to any of those questions is yes, you need to think about it. Let us look to the word for clarity. It says in Jeremiah 17:5 that you will be cursed if your trust is totally in man, because when that happens, your heart is departing from God. There is no time to see you God's way, if your focus is on another man's perspective of you. The way you feel about how people perceive you is connected to the way you see yourself and view your circumstances as well. It is all wrapped into one big package. Sometimes we are so focused on who we want people to think we are we truly forget who we really are. That is why God reminded us not to let our trust be totally with man, so that we would know how to handle people and their perspectives and perceptions. He wanted to make sure that we knew that He is the only one we should always rely on. He has placed people in your life to help you, but if you rely on them too much, you will be disappointed every time. It is totally different when you have to make a decision that stays in line with the word and you need assistance. Proverbs 11:14 states, *"Where no counsel is, the people fall: but in the multitude of counselors there is safety."* In order to remain balanced you have to allow some people to speak into your life at different times. However, they should not be your only source. As long as you are not solely depending on the opinions of people, godly counsel can be beneficial. Godly counsel is the healthy way to listen to others. The flip side to that is letting people's opinions control you. This is very unhealthy. In order to be certain that their perceptions and perspectives do not steer you in the wrong direction, we must look at it two ways: godly and ungodly perceptions. We will look at examples in the word of God that gives us guidelines on how the men of the Bible dealt with the godly and ungodly counsel of people and how it affected their view.

Moses' brother Aaron was one of the first people in the Bible to allow people's perspectives to change his perception of God. Aaron was in charge of the Israelites when Moses went up to meet with God for forty days and nights. God clearly stated to the children of Israel that they were not to worship idols or other gods (see Exodus 34:17). Aaron knew that Moses was going to worship God, but did not know how long it would take. When the people began to press him for answers, he did not know what to say. He forgot what God called him to do, and let the people's complaints override what God said. He began to allow them to choose for him. They believed Moses would not return and did not know God well enough to trust

Him. Aaron saw himself in the same position as the people. He took all of their jewelry, melted it and created a molten calf. He commanded the people to worship and make sacrifices to it. Aaron disobeyed God because the people complained that they could see no God and needed something to worship. At that moment, all he could see was that people were upset and needed comfort. He neglected that the very thing that God told him not to do was what the people were asking of him. Their counsel came from the wrong perspective. It did not include God's will. The people were only thinking of themselves. Consequently, Aaron, nor his sons, succeeded Moses in leadership. Therefore, it is truly unhealthy to let what people think or say change your perception. You lose your position. God promoted someone else who could see things the way He does and who did not care so much for the people that they would change his view of where God placed him. That is important. God has to know that He can trust you not to let people sway you. We are all guilty of allowing people to do that to us, no matter how severe.

I loved my family so much, that I would do anything to make them happy. Even if it meant I had to be unhappy, I wanted to make sure that I pleased them. I lived with my grandmother and aunts my entire life, because my mother did not live in a positive environment. As I stated before, my father was in the air force. He was stationed in South Carolina. I chose to live with my mother's relatives; however, it was not much better than living with my mother. Because of our situation, my sisters and I were treated poorly. We were expected to be grateful for the things that were done for us, even though they all came with a price. You paid for the sins of your parents. My mother was not in the place they thought she should be, so they figured we would grow up to be just like her. In their eyes we would never be anything.

I started to believe everything they said. I just wanted to please them. I wanted to feel like I belonged. If you are not sure of your position, then you will start to believe about yourself what people feel about you. Like I did, you will do everything you can to please them. The word even tells us that the man's eyes are never satisfied (Proverbs 27:20). So how could you even begin to keep any person happy? We are not supposed to because joy comes from God. The one thing I learned is that not everyone will be happy with you no matter what you do.

I was finally able to gain an understanding of what Jesus meant when he talked about "casting your pearls". God used this scripture to enlighten me on why it is so important not to let even my family's perceptions control me. Matthew 7:6 says, *"Do not give what is holy to dogs and do not throw your pearls before swine, or they will trample them under their feet, and turn and tear you to pieces."* The revelation God gave me on this scripture was that pearls are the gifts He has given us. A pearl, by definition, is a smooth, lustrous, variously colored deposit formed in the shells of certain mollusks and valued as gems. Swine, not the pig, is defined as a brutish or contemptible person. This also means entirely physical or lacking reason or intelligence. Jesus is explaining that God has put something of great worth and value on the inside of you. People who do not understand what God is doing in your life will abuse the gifts He placed inside of you. This includes family members. The last part of the scripture says that they will "tear you apart". This means that they will have you in so many different directions trying to keep them happy. They think they know who you will become, so they treat you the way they see you. This can be the same for church family and other people that are in your life. They are not able to attest to what your true gifts and talents are. A lot of the time past experiences, alter their present expectations of what they perceive as your potential. The problem is that no one knows everything about you and they forget that it was God who created you. It is not their fault; it is just not their assignment. I did not know God well enough to disregard their feelings. After all they were the ones who raised me. I figured if anyone could tell me who I was, my family could. If you listen to people long enough, your perception starts to become what they think. If a negative person tells you that you will never become the man or woman of God He created you to be, and you do not know yourself, you will believe them. You will end up forfeiting the plan of God for your life. That is why Aaron could not stand up to the people he had co-labored with in Egypt. He did not know who he was.

Another example about ungodly counsel was the story of King Saul. Saul was a man of great stature. God sent the prophet Samuel to anoint him king over Israel (see I Samuel 10). Saul was able to do great things for God once the spirit came upon him. However, Saul was more concerned with what the people wanted. He based his perception of himself on what people said or felt about him. When confronted by Samuel about his mistakes, he was arrogant and blamed the people (see I Samuel 15). As I stated in the previous chapter, you cannot blame anyone for your decisions except yourself. If you allow people to lead you astray, God is not going to come looking for them, you are responsible for your outcome. God eventually removed His mantle from Saul and gave it to another more worthy of the call. Can you see the pattern here?

In both examples, the men lost their position. They allowed the way people viewed them to change their view of God. These two men cared more about what the people saw than what the God who called them said. When that happens, you lose the reverential fear of God that you should have. You diminish His power, when we do not obey His commandments. When I say diminish His power, I do not mean God is not still powerful, I mean the power of God in your life. You cut yourself off. When you attach your perspective and perception to those of people who do not have relationship with God, you destroy your own destiny.

Chapter Six

"Where there is no counsel, the people fall; but in the multitude of counselors there is safety" (Proverbs 11:14).

There are times where sound godly counsel from people is good. Godly counsel is sound advice based on the principles laid out for us in God's word. The Bible states in Proverbs 11:14 that, *"Where there is no counsel, the people fall; but in the multitude of counselors there is safety."* That means godly counsel, not someone who does not even read God's word. Let me clarify that statement, God can use anyone He wants to speak into your life, but you have to make sure it lines up with His word. You have to know for yourself if the counsel you are receiving is confirmation or just not in context at all. When it is Godly counsel, it lines up with what you are doing or seeing at that time. Moses and his father-in-law shared some godly counsel that allowed the plan of God to flow. Let us look at this situation.

Moses and his father-in-law had a great relationship. Jethro took Moses in at the time when he was running from his past and gave him his oldest daughter to wed. When God spoke to Moses, letting him know his purpose, Jethro was in agreement with what the man had to do. Moses received wisdom from Jethro (see Exodus 18:7-11).

As the leader of the children of Israel, Moses had many responsibilities. He was in the position of leader, minister, and judge over them. This was a demanding position for him, because he did everything himself. Aaron and his family were the priests, but ultimately the bulk of responsibility God gave to Moses. Moses wanted to hear all the cases of the people, but Jethro persuaded him to delegate responsibility to others so he would not burn himself out (see Exodus 18). Moses saw that this was a good idea and assigned leaders from each tribe to handle the simple things, while he still judged the complicated issues (see Exodus 18:25-26). Jethro had Moses' welfare in mind when he gave him that counsel. The consequences were favorable, because Jethro was able to see clearly that Moses needed to delegate responsibility. That would not only take that burden off him, he would be able to spend more time with God. Now that sounds like good counsel to me. That sets you up to see God even more in every situation Any advice you receive from someone that points you in the direction of the Father is sound godly counsel. The opposite is true for ungodly counsel.

In my family going to church was as a routine for some and special occasion for others. As I began to seek God for a closer relationship, and my perspective on life began to change, my family would try to keep me in the old mindset. They would say things like "You spend too much time in church" and "Why are you always talking about the Lord?" Conversations with them always focused around others and when I refused to be a part of it or changed the subject they did not understand. They would also try to make me think that even walking with God, things would not change. I would always hear about the "curses" on our family and things of that nature. For them that may have been true, however, my perception of my life and the people in my life changed. Even though the circumstances and the people may have been the same, my outlook changed. I began to block out their counsel and turn to focus on the people God sent me for encouragement. It was not easy at first, but I eventually drifted away from my old way of seeing things and allowed the spirit of God to rest. God began to unlock all of the hidden potential and uproot some things in me. His word was my road map for my life. You see people cannot tell you anything about yourself that God has not already revealed within you. I had to learn that. It took me a long time to block out the negative outlook. My family either accepted and respected my walk or just ignored me altogether. We all have situations where we still allow the way others see us, affect our view. I have and I know I am not alone. We have to be willing to forsake the opinions of those who do not have God's perspective.

If you find yourself allowing the way that people view you, or God, override your own view you may want to step back and take inventory of your priorities. Step away and seek the face of God. He will guide you. He will even show you from whom you are to seek counsel. The word lets us know that the man who does not follow the counsel of ungodly people and sit in the seat of those who mock God (people who do not have a clue what God's perspective is) is blessed (see Psalm 1). To let you know how true that is, I will show you another example of a man of God who looked at things from God's perspective. He did not allow others perception to change how he felt or acted towards God.

David, as explained earlier, was a man after God's own heart. He worshipped, prayed, and fasted to God regardless of what people felt. He was the king and did not care how people felt about his relationship with God. His wife, Saul's daughter, Michal despised the fact that he praised God until his clothing fell from his body (see II Samuel 6). David responded to her in

II Samuel 6:21-22 stating, *"It was before the Lord, which chose me before thy father, and before his entire house to appoint me ruler over the people of the Lord, over Israel: therefore I will play before the Lord. And I will be viler than this, and will be base in my own sight: and of the maidservants which thou hast spoken of, of them shall I be had in honor."* David was bold enough to let Michal know that he would praise the Lord regardless of what people think. He even went as far to let her know that even the house cleaners and servants she was speaking of not respecting him, would still respect and honor him as king. That was his perspective, exactly the way that God would have looked at the situation. Why would you care if people thought less of you because you were praising God until your clothes fell off? They would have the problem, not you. Let them question you. David was so happy that the Ark of the Lord was back in his possession that he could not help, but to dance before the Lord. If I were Michal, I would have joined David. She was too busy despising him for something she was not bold enough to do. In many other instances, David would separate himself from everyone to seek the Lord as well. He knew that God kept him alive. Before every battle, he would ask God for His perception of the outcome. God would always steer David in the right direction. That is counsel directly from God.

When you have relationship like that with the Father, it should not matter who has a problem with you. What I have learned, and still in the process of learning, is that the reason why people criticize you is that they are unhappy with themselves.

David knew that praising God was an outward show of the love that he had for his Father. He understood that the people Michal spoke of could not judge him. All they could do was respect his relationship with God. If they did not respect his praise, that was their loss. Michal was barren because of her lack of respect for her husband (see 2 Samuel 6:23). You see. David just told her what the deal was and because of her lack of obedience to her husband, she missed out.

As I stated before, people only have the control you allow them to have over your perception. God has given us power over all flesh (see John 17:2), so why would he allow people to control us? That is not of God. This scripture tells us that we even have power over ourselves. We are made of flesh. We have the power to control how we see the way people see us. However, we can only exercise this power when we utilize the Spirit of God in us. We need to keep our focus on the one who created us, so that we can see like him.

Part Three Discussion Questions

(Chapters 5 & 6)

Please answer all questions completely. They are designed to help you and will only be beneficial if you answer truthfully.

1) Do you rely on other people's opinions and expectations of you more than Gods? Has this hindered your growth?

2) What is your definition of counsel as it relates to Proverbs 11:14? What does this scripture mean to you?

3) Have you listened to someone else on an important matter and regret doing so? (Give an example of this and how God fixed the situation.)

4) Has someone given you very good counsel and it helped you greatly? (Please explain)

5) How can you allow the word of God to help you stand when others do not understand what God has called

you to do? (Please explain in detail and use scripture

references.)

IV.

How To See From

God's Perspective

Chapter Seven

"...I am the light of the world: he that follows me shall not walk in darkness, but shall have the light of life" (John 8:12).

Have you ever found yourself trying to walk through a room without turning on the light? It is one of the most difficult tasks. Especially if there is no light coming from anywhere. You can trip over things you forgot were in certain places. Things even appear differently in the dark. The smallest objects are difficult to find, and you see things from the wrong perspective. You have to allow your eyes to adjust to the darkness in an attempt to make out what is in the room. Even then, you still are unable to see clearly. What happens when you turn on the light? There is nothing hidden from your view. Your perspective has changed from seeing nothing to seeing everything. You can now see the coat hanging in the closet that looked like a person and that shawl draped over a chair that looked like something else. If you never turned the light on your perspective of the room would be distorted. Once the light comes on, you can see what is really going on. That is how we should view our relationship with God. God wants us to walk in the light so that we can see as He does. So turn on the light.

Your relationship with someone depicts how you perceive that person.   Before you truly know a person, you make assumptions based on surface perceptions of who they are. You are totally in the dark about their true personality. Once you get closer to them, you learn more about them and the way you then perceive them depends on what you have learned. The same is so with God.   Before we develop a relationship with God, we see everything in darkness.   After we come to know Him, we are able to see everything from His view.   I know   we   talked   about   seeing   ourselves   from   God's perspective, but this is even deeper than that. Jesus explained in the heading scripture that He is the light of the world. If we follow that light, we will see everything, including ourselves, the way that God sees us.

Let us look at the story preceding this particular verse for a moment. Jesus had just assisted the woman accused of adultery by the Scribes and Pharisees. These men were attempting to stone the woman for the sins she had committed, but were unwilling to see their own faults. Okay picture this. Everyone is standing in place, ready to throw his stone at this adulterous woman. "She deserves to be put to death" and "She's no good" some might say. The men sought Jesus so that He would help them to justify why they should take her life. They placed the woman before Jesus and made sure that they explained the law God gave to Moses (John 8:3-4). Jesus, God in the form of man, looking at this from the right perspective told them that the person who had no sin at all should throw the first stone at the woman. That was it. He did not go into a long drawn out argument about the terrible sin of committing adultery. He simply stated a fact and continued writing in the sand. When he looked up and saw that they were gone, He told her to go and sin no more (see John 8:11). He asked her if any of them condemned her and when she said no, He told her He would not either. The only command was to "go and sin no more".

I know you may be wondering what this story has to do with perspective and perception. I will explain. First I want to look at some key things in this situation. Did you notice that she was on trial alone? I am most certain that some of the men she had been sleeping with were holding the stones. It takes more than one person to commit an act of adultery. The perspective of the men involved was that they were exempt from punishment. This came from what they perceived true relationship with God to be. They figured that because they go to the temple to pray and show others that they are fasting, they are exempt from the law. They still lived under the law and feel that as long as they sacrifice a goat or some other animal; they are seen as righteous in the eyes of God.

Therefore, they are convinced that if you do all those things, you are saved and going to heaven no matter what. Since the woman (the sinner) cheated, that gives them the right to take her life. After all, she is just a sinner. Wrong! Sin is sin. God sees it all as dirt. That is why Jesus said what "He without sin should throw the first stone". He was the only one that could have done that, but chose to love this woman in spite of what she had done. We have to see what He sees. He wants us to be able to look at ourselves before we condemn others. He wants us to be real with Him when we are in relationship with Him. He already knows what you did. He wants to know if you can see it the way He does.

I know you are saying, "Well we all have sinned and fallen short of God's glory, but once you accept Him you should know better." That is your opinion. As I stated in previous chapters, we are not perfect. He does not expect that from us. That is why we should be quick to show mercy. Nevertheless, if we are to walk with God and have the right perception in life, we must make sure that we are seeing everything clearly.

The only way to ensure that we are doing this is to check in with God all the time. The prayer should be "God what do you want to do in my life today?" In addition to that, "How can I make what I did on yesterday better?" It is like taking off your glasses, which are fogged up or stained with tears that have now dried up, wiping them off, and then putting them back on again. Is that better? It works for me. That is exactly what looking at life from God's perspective does for me. I notice in my own life that when my vision is cloudy, I cannot hear clearly from God. What I mean is if so many things are clogging my mind, He cannot get through to me. I can only see what is happening right now and the bigger picture is so far out of my view. If there is a situation in which someone must be to blame, I am unable to assess my side if I am not seeing clearly. We have to constantly stay in a mode of repentance to make sure that we are not thinking that we have done nothing wrong. Try not to be upset with someone when they tell you that you are not seeing the way God would see the situation. My husband and I have to help each other all the time with this. Sometimes I may be so caught up in a situation and he, being able to see from the outside in, says "Honey just step outside of it because you are only seeing things this or that way and you're making it out to be more or less than what it is." I do the same for him. That is where God is standing. He is outside of the situation. Because He can see the big picture of your life, He is able to show you things from a higher place.

In Isaiah 55:8, He let us know that His thoughts are higher than ours. It is like when you are a child and you have a train set. The tracks are set on this replica of a town or city. From where you stand, you can see everything. You can even see things on the tracks that may cause the train to derail. You can remove the object so that the ride will continue smoothly for the train. That is the perspective from which God sees your life. He can remove things that will hinder you. That also means His perception comes from a place we can only attempt to reach by continually sitting at His feet.

I would like to give you another example in reference to our perspective of relationship with God. In Luke 18:10- it reads,

"Two men went up into the temple to pray; one a Pharisee, and the other a publican. The Pharisee stood and prayed thus with himself, God I thank thee, that I am not as other men are, extortionists, unjust, adulterers, or even as this publican. I fast twice in the week; I give tithes of all that I possess. And the publican, standing afar off, would not lift up so much as his eyes unto heaven, but smote upon his breast, saying, God be merciful to me a sinner. I tell you, this man went down to his house justified rather than the other: For every one that exalts himself shall be abased; and he that humbles himself shall be exalted."

Do you find yourself thinking like the Pharisee? On the other hand, are you more like the publican? Which man should you identify with? Let's look at the Pharisee first in this scripture. He saw himself as a wonderful, powerful prayer warrior who did everything according to the laws of God. He saw himself as the perfect saint. Equating that to what we deal with now, he was all that and some chips with dip. He came to church faithfully every time the doors were opened. He stood before "God" in the temple and prayed for others that they would be as good as him. He condemned people who did not live or do things the way he did. Oh, he had it all together. Nobody but God himself could speak to this man about anything. He kept score of all the things he did so that later he could stand before God and give an account of them. Sound familiar to you? We are all guilty of it. Now do not misunderstand, God wants us to see ourselves after his image and likeness (see Genesis 1:26). He just does not want us to get the wrong idea about it. We are to follow the example of Jesus, but not to pat ourselves on the back for doing so. It is not of God. It is a requirement, not an accomplishment. When we start to stick our noses up at others for what we feel they are not doing correctly, we have stepped into another place that does not include God. We have totally lost focus of what is important if that is the case.

Now the publican, on the other hand, does not give God his time or money. The publican was not even able to look up to God, because of his sins. He counted it a privilege to be in the God's presence, not an obligation. He represents the people who have not been in church all their lives, and looking for something more than just church. He is willing to look at his faults and bring them to God so that he can be set free. This person may not be wearing the latest outfits, or drive the best vehicle. They may not even have great living conditions. They want to be transparent before their Creator and repent for the sin that has separated them from him. These are the people who come to church to cultivate their relationship with God and not for status. They don't care about titles or how people feel about them.

The first man was only seeing things from his perspective. He could only see all the good things that he was doing for God. He was doing God a favor by praying, fasting, and giving. He was so full of himself that he even had the nerve to look down on his brother standing next to him. In contrast, the publican was so broken that all he could see was God. He just wanted to ask forgiveness for his sins. He saw himself as a sinner who wanted to change. Even if he had been in relationship with God, he was repenting of his sin so that nothing would come between them.

The heart that the second man had is what God is looking for from us. If we are to clearly see what He has for us to do, we must remove ourselves from the equation. We must be willing to endure shame and embarrassment for the glory of God. It should be so much about Him that we check in with Him on everything before we step out. Just like in a natural relationship you want to talk with someone everyday or often to make sure that your relationship is intact. This is what God desires from us. He desires for us to love what He loves and hate what He hates. He detests sin in any form. He wants to commune with us without the blockage of sin. Just like water flows freely through a stream, He wants his presence to flow through us. The only time that water is unable to keep flowing, is if something stops it. The only way that we lose our connection with God is if something is blocking our view of Him. Surrender your life to Him today and allow Him to show you what He sees about you.

Part Four Discussion Questions

(Chapter 7)

Please answer all questions completely. They are designed to help you and will only be beneficial if you answer truthfully.

1) How do you see God? Do you have a personal relationship with Him?

2) What is your definition of the word "relationship"?

3) Were you able to relate to the Pharisee or the publican in this Chapter? (Please explain)

4) How can you cultivate your relationship with God? Are you assured of His love for you?

CAN YOU SEE CLEARLY NOW?

After you have released the old feelings of shame, regret, and rejection, how do you see yourself? Are you so full of pride that you pray selfish prayers unto God like this Pharisee? Alternatively, do you find yourself condemning others for the same things that you do as the other religious men who wanted to stone the woman? Do you see yourself as a work in progress, even after you have come into relationship with God? How do you view those circumstances now? Has your perspective of God now changed?

Check your spectacles and make sure that you are seeing from the right perspective. If you find that you are not seeing correctly, change your perception, so that God can mold you. It is only at the moment you realize your vision is off, that you will recognize the need for God. We must be first willing to accept that we are all works in progress. We are constantly in a mode of preparation so that we can move into the new levels

God has for all of us. Find out where you are right now in your walk with God, so that you will know how to view everything that comes towards you. Let God be the final authority no matter what.

If you have not accepted God's view, find out what is hindering you. The word of God states in John 16:13 that "the spirit of God will guide you into all truth". There is freedom in that truth. That includes the truth about you, circumstances, people, and true relationship with God. So at whatever level you are on in your life right now make a conscious choice to allow the power, perspective, and perception of God to guide your life. I stand in agreement with you right now for that to happen for you. I pray that the Lord will bless you for seeking to view things through His eyes. Amen.

PRAYER OF SALVATION

It would be very difficult to have your view changed by someone you have no relationship with or do not value. I would like to take this opportunity to conclude this book by introducing you to the one that changed my view forever. He is the only true and living God. If you are reading this book and have never given your life to Jesus Christ or even experienced a true relationship with him then this is your time. You have probably heard about him but your view of Him was congested with your imperfections. This can keep you from allowing yourself a true experience with Jesus Christ. However the good news is that the bible declares that if you confess with your mouth the Lord Jesus, and believe in your heart that God has raised him from the dead, you shall be saved. So repeat this prayer with me so God can begin to transform your view of life, "Father in the name of Jesus, I come before you today, confessing that I have sinned against you. I repent of my sins this day and I believe that you sent your Son Jesus Christ who shed his blood and died for my sins on the cross. And on the third day he rose again so that I could receive power and life everlasting. This day I accept Him as my Lord and Savior. Please come into my life, change my heart and change my view, that I can have the mind of Christ, in Jesus name I pray. Amen

ABOUT THE AUTHOR

Jeaketa Manga is an author, psalmist, and minister of the gospel. Born and raised in Petersburg, Virginia, she is the oldest of six siblings. She recently obtained her Bachelor of Science in Marketing at Virginia Commonwealth University. Jeaketa has learned to overcome a lot of the struggles she endured through reading, studying, and applying the word in her life. She has learned to change her outlook through the situations that have occurred in her life and wants to share with others how to let God get the glory out of everything that you do.

Jeaketa and her husband, Kennedy, currently attend Mt. Gilead Full Gospel International Ministries, under the leadership of Bishop Daniel and Co-Pastor Elena Robertson. There she serves on the Excellence Choir and Praise & Worship ministry.

Jeaketa and her husband currently reside in Chesterfield, Virginia. They are the blessed parents of one child, Kaitlyn Nicole.

91

You can obtain additional copies of

LORD CHANGE MY VIEW

To order and to obtain discounts on orders of 10 or more copies for individuals and/or organizations or for booking information on Jeaketa Manga please call:804-426-9692 or visit us on the web@

www.destinygrouppublishing.com

www.ingramcontent.com/pod-product-compliance
Lightning Source LLC
Chambersburg PA
CBHW020920090426
42736CB00008B/718